Stalking the Perfect Tan

Doonesbury books by G. B. Trudeau

Still a Few Bugs in the System
The President Is a Lot Smarter Than You Think
But This War Had Such Promise
Call Me When You Find America
Guilty, Guilty, Guilty!
"What Do We Have for the Witnesses, Johnnie?"
Dare To Be Great, Ms. Caucus
Wouldn't a Gremlin Have Been More Sensible?
"Speaking of Inalienable Rights, Amy..."
You're Never Too Old for Nuts and Berries
An Especially Tricky People
As the Kid Goes for Broke
Stalking the Perfect Tan

Stalking the Perfect Tan

a *Doonesbury* book by G. B. Trudeau

Holt, Rinehart and Winston
New York

YOU MEAN, VENTURA'S ALREADY CLEARED OUT?

NO, NO, IT'S JUST MY TRANSITIONAL OFFICE! BUT IT'S GOT A **GREAT** VIEW OF THE CAPITOL!

IT'S **JUST** SO EXCITING, DICK! OH, AND GUESS WHAT?! WE'VE BEEN INVITED TO GAIL HOWE'S FOR DINNER TONIGHT!

WHO'S GAIL HOWE?

GAIL HOWE? DICK, SHE ONLY PRESIDES OVER THE MOST BREATHLESSLY "A" LIST SALON IN WASHINGTON!

I'LL PASS. "WILD KINGDOM"'S ON TONIGHT.

SWEETEST! THERE'LL BE WALL-TO-WALL SECRETARIES-DESIGNATE!

GBTrudeau

EXCUSE ME, MISS. BRENDA NICKS FROM "PEOPLE" SENT ME OVER..

OH, YES, MR. REDFERN! WE'VE BEEN EXPECTING YOU, SIR!

WILL YOU BE ATTENDING THE FULL WEEK OF PEOPLE SEMINAR TRAINING, MR. REDFERN?

I'M AFRAID SO.

OKEY DOKE! WELL, I THINK WE'VE GOT EVERYTHING HERE.. OH, YES, COULD YOU TELL ME WHO YOU'RE SLEEPING WITH NOW?

I BEG YOUR PARDON?

ANYONE FAMOUS? IT'S FOR YOUR NAME TAG.

SAY, GINNY, WHERE IS CLYDE, ANYWAY? WASN'T HE SUPPOSED TO BE JOINING US?

YEAH, BUT HE SAID HE HAD TO GET OVER TO THE LIBRARY. HE AND BENNY HAVE A NEW PROJECT..

I DON'T SUPPOSE IT'S "ROOTS"-RELATED..

AFRAID SO.

GBTrudeau

FIGURED OUT WHO YOUR FATHER WAS YET, CLYDE?

WATCH YOUR MOUTH, MAN!

SO HOW GOES THE SEARCH FOR YOUR LATE GREATS, CLYDE?

SLOW, MAN, REAL SLOW..

BUT THAT'S TO BE EXPECTED. HELL, IT TOOK BROTHER HALEY MOST OF **TWELVE** YEARS TO CHECK OUT HIS ROOTS!

BESIDES, THIS COULD VERY WELL PAY OFF BIG! WHO KNOWS, MAN — I MIGHT BE RELATED TO SOME VERY HEAVY ETHIOPIAN EMPEROR!

ON THE OTHER HAND, YOU MIGHT BE RELATED TO IDI AMIN.

NOT A CHANCE, MAN! WELL, MAYBE MOM'S SIDE..

WHITE HOUSE SYMBOLS. DELACOURT SPEAKING.

DUANE? THIS IS HAM HERE..

I'VE JUST BEEN IN TO SEE JIMMY! HE'S **VERY** PLEASED WITH YOUR WORK, DUANE! THE CALL-IN SHOW, THE CHAT, THE CARDIGAN, THE LIMO CUTS, FULL FINANCIAL DISCLOSURE, AMY'S "TRUSTY" GOVERNESS —ALL UN-EQUIVOCAL HITS!

FACT IS, DUANE, YOUR WORK HAS BECOME TOO IMPORTANT FOR ONLY A SUBCABINET OPERATION! THE PRESIDENT WANTS TO NOMINATE YOU TO A NEW POST—SECRETARY OF SYMBOLISM! WHAT DO YOU SAY, BUDDY?

OKAY BY ME. I DON'T HAVE TO TAKE A PAY RAISE, DO I?

HECK, NO! IN FACT, I'M SURE YOU'VE GOT A CUT COMING TO YOU!

GB Trudeau

GOOD EVENING. TODAY THE PRESIDENT CREATED A NEW ADMINISTRATION POST — SECRETARY OF SYMBOLISM. OUR MAN CAROL SIMPSON WAS THERE.

TO ADMINISTRATION TOPSIDERS, IT CAME AS NO SURPRISE TODAY THAT CARTER PICKED DUANE DELACOURT TO BE HIS NEW SYMBOLISM CHIEF. HE WAS, AFTER ALL, THE MAN BEHIND THE CARDIGAN, THE CHAT, THE STROLL, AND THE PUBLIC EDUCATION OF AMY!

THE SECRETARY-DESIGNATE IS NOTHING IF NOT PROLIFIC. DELACOURT HAS ALREADY ANNOUNCED THAT A MAJOR SYMBOLIC GESTURE WILL TAKE PLACE TONIGHT AT 9:00 P.M. EASTERN STANDARD TIME.

NBC NEWS WILL, OF COURSE, BE PROVIDING LIVE COVERAGE OF THE GESTURE. FOR CAPITOL HILL REACTION, THIS FROM OUR MAN LINDA ELLERBEE..

GOOD EVENING. PRESIDENT CARTER'S NOMINEE FOR SEC- RETARY OF SYMBOLISM, DUANE DELACOURT, HAS GOTTEN OFF TO A RUNNING START.

SPEAKING AT A SPECIAL PRESS CONFERENCE LAST NIGHT, THE SEC- RETARY-DESIGNATE ANNOUNCED HE WOULD BE HOLDING REGULAR PHONE-A-THONS TO ASK AVERAGE AMERICANS WHAT SYMBOLS THEY WOULD MOST LIKE TO SEE IN THE CARTER ADMINISTRATION.

TODAY DUANE DELACOURT HELD HIS FIRST SUCH PHONE-A-THON AND NBC NEWS WAS THERE..

HELLO?

HELLO! THIS IS YOUR SECRETARY OF SYMBOLISM!

YEAH, I'D LIKE TO SEE MORE PHONE-A- THONS.

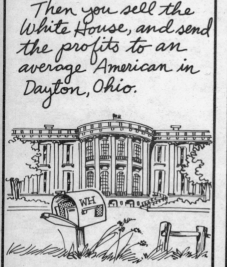

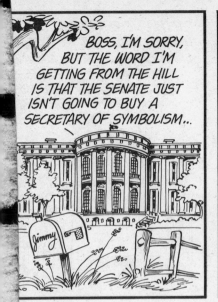

MR. DELACOURT, MY POINT IS THAT JIMMY CARTER HAS HAD **YEARS** OF PUBLIC SERVICE TO FIND OUT WHAT'S ON THE MINDS OF THE AMERICAN PEOPLE!

IF THE PRESIDENT DOESN'T KNOW WHAT THE NEEDS OF THE COUNTRY ARE BY NOW, HE'S **NEVER** GOING TO KNOW!

SENATOR, AS I SAID BEFORE, IT'S REALLY A QUESTION OF KEEPING IN TOUCH..

KEEPING IN **TOUCH?!** MR. DELACOURT, THE MAN NEVER LET **GO!** FIVE MONTHS AFTER THE ELECTION, HE'S **STILL** CAMPAIGNING!

WELL, WE FEEL VOTERS APPRECIATE THE FACT HE CARES ENOUGH TO CAMPAIGN AFTER THE ELECTION AS WELL.

BUT, DUANE! HE **WON!** HE **WON** THE ELECTION!

I KNOW. I STILL CAN'T BELIEVE IT. IT'S LIKE A DREAM, Y'KNOW?

MOVING ON TO THE LATIN AMERICAN DIVISION, HERE TO PRESENT OUR NEXT HUMAN RIGHTS AWARD IS A CERTAIN LOCAL PROFESSOR OF DIPLOMACY!

WOULD YOU PLEASE GIVE A VERY WARM WELCOME TO OUR OWN NOBEL PEACE PRIZE-WINNING **DR. HENRY KISSINGER!**

HA! HA! HA! HA! **HA!**

I.. I.. DON'T BELIEVE IT!

HA, HA! OH, HOW AWFUL! HOW CYNICAL!

THANK YOU. THE AWARD FOR THE FEWEST CURFEWS IN A TWELVE MONTH PERIOD..

MUST BE A TOWN-GOWN GESTURE..

HONESTLY THIS ADMINISTRATION JUST KILLS ME.

GBTrudeau

NOW, JOANIE, WHAT'S ALL THIS NONSENSE ABOUT YOU ACTUALLY BECOMING A LAWYER?..

WELL, IT'S TRUE, ZONK! I'M GRADUATING FROM BOALT ON SATURDAY!

BUT, JOANIE, THAT'S..*CRAZY!* DO YOU HAVE ANY IDEA WHAT IT'S *LIKE* OUT THERE?

NO, NOT REALLY. BUT THAT'S WHY I'M LOOKING FORWARD TO IT SO MUCH ..

ZONKER, IT'S TIME I STOPPED PREPARING FOR MY LIFE, AND STARTED GETTING ON WITH IT! I FEEL READY TO ACCEPT THE RESPONSIBILITY OF THE CHOICES I'VE MADE, TO FACE MY FUTURE SQUARELY!

EASY, JOANIE, EASY! YOU'RE BECOMING HYSTERICAL!

MY MIND'S MADE UP, ZONKER..

YOU KNOW, RICK, YOUR MENTIONING THE ETHICS COMMITTEE GOT ME THINKING. LACEY DAVENPORT'S ON THAT COMMITTEE. THINK SHE'D BE HIRING COUNSEL FOR THE KOREAN HEARINGS?

WELL, IT'S WORTH A TRY..

EXCEPT IT COULD BE RISKY. MAYBE SHE'S NOT ABOVE HARBORING POLITICAL GRUDGES, YOU KNOW?

I MEAN, WHAT IF SHE HIRES ME, AND THEN LEAKS SOMETHING AND BLAMES ME, AND THEN FIRES ME ON NATIONAL TELEVISION, **HUMILIATING** ME IN FRONT OF THE WHOLE COUNTRY?

YEAH, WHAT IF SHE DOES THAT?

I BETTER NOT CALL HER.

GBTrudeau

MS. CAUCUS, WHAT A DELIGHT TO HEAR FROM YOU! ARE YOU HERE IN WASHINGTON?

UM.. YES, I AM, MRS. DAVENPORT! JUST GOT IN, SO I THOUGHT, HEC WHY NOT GIVE MY CONGRESSWOMAN A CALL, YOU KNOW, TO SHOW THERE WERE NO HARD FEELINGS ABOUT LAST FALL..

IN FACT, BOTH GINNY AND I FEEL IT WAS RATHER A PRIVILEGE TO RUN AGAINST YOU. IT WAS A CLEAN RACE, RIGHT? AND FREE OF ACRIMONY! AND..UH..WELL FOUGHT BY BOTH SIDES, DON'T YOU THINK?

YES, I GUESS IT WAS, DEAR..

LACEY, I NEED A JOB.

SO DID I, DEAR. BUT COME BY ANY-WAY.

MY DEAR MS. CAUCUS! YOU ARE A WONDER! HARD AT WORK ALREADY!

THE CHIEF COUNSEL SENT ME DOWN HERE, LACEY. HE WANTS ME TO FAMILIARIZE MYSELF WITH SOME OF THE DOCUMENTARY EVIDENCE!

WHAT DO YOU THINK SO FAR?

WELL, I'M JUST AMAZED! I HAD NO IDEA THERE WERE SO MANY REPUTATIONS AT STAKE!

THAT'S RIGHT. THAT'S WHY THE HEARINGS ARE SO SENSITIVE!

YOU KNOW, I CAN'T BELIEVE I'M FERRETING OUT CORRUPTION ON MY FIRST DAY!

CAREFUL, NOW, DEAR! THAT'S FOR THE FEDS TO DECIDE.

GBTrudeau

I THINK YOU'LL LIKE MY SPEECH, HONEY. IT'S FULL OF SURPRISES, VERY MUCH IN THE ANDREW YOUNG TRADITION.

SURPRISES, SIR?

YOU KNOW, WE PROFESSIONAL DIPLOMATS OWE A GREAT DEBT OF THANKS TO ANDY! HE PAVED THE WAY FOR A WHOLE NEW STYLE OF IMPROVISATIONAL DIPLOMACY!

BECAUSE OF HIM, TODAY'S NEW ENVOYS CAN FLOAT WHATEVER VIEWS THEY WANT, EVEN IF THEY DIRECTLY CONTRADICT STATE DEPARTMENT POLICY!

YOU SURE ABOUT THAT, SIR?

POSITIVE! HONEY, I COULD START A WAR HERE TONIGHT, AND CY WOULD BACK ME UP!

UM.. SIR, COULD I CHECK THAT OVER FOR SPELLING?

LEONARD WOODCOCK! I JUST CAN'T GET OVER IT! WHAT *EVER* COULD HAVE POSSESSED CARTER TO PICK WOODCOCK FOR CHINA?

WELL, SIR, MAYBE IT'S BECAUSE MR. WOODCOCK'S CAREER HAS BEEN ONE OF GREAT SENSITIVITY TO THE PLIGHT OF THE WORKING CLASS

HONEY, *ALL LABOR LEADERS* ARE SENSITIVE TO THE WORKING CLASS! THAT'S HOW THEY AVOID BELONGING TO IT!

BUT DIDN'T HE TAKE ON THE GANG OF THREE, SIR?

THAT'S THE *BIG* THREE AND NEXT T YOU PEOPLE THOSE GUYS ARE PUSS CATS!

ANYWAY, WENNER WON'T EVEN RETURN MY CALLS, SO I GUESS A JOB AT "ROLLING STONE" IS OUT...

AMAZING! AFTER ALL YOU'VE BEEN THROUGH, YOU'D THINK HE'D AT LEAST LEND A HAND!

NOPE. HE NEEDS THEM BOTH FOR SOCIAL CLIMBING. AND YOURS TRULY IS NOT EXACTLY "A" LIST ANYMORE. BUT WHO CARES? I GOT OTHER PLANS!

OH, YEAH? LIKE WHAT?

A FANTASTIC BUSINESS OPPORTUNITY! SOMETHING I'VE BEEN TOYING WITH FOR YEARS!

NOT THE TRAINING CENTER FOR ATTACK DOGS?

NO, NO, BETTER! REMEMBER THAT LITTLE MASSAGE PARLOR I HAD MY EYE ON?..

THE ONE WITH THE BOWLING LANES?

GB Trudeau

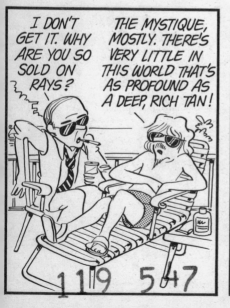